AM I TOO QUIET?

P.S. NO, YOU'RE NOT.

A HOW-TO GUIDE TO USING YOUR QUIETNESS TO YOUR ADVANTAGE

YADIRICHI OYIBO

Am I Too Quiet? P.S. No, You're Not. A How-To Guide To Using Your Quietness To Your Advantage.

Copyright © 2022 by Yadirichi Oyibo

Paperback ISBN 979-8-4115-3381-1
Hardcover ISBN 979-8-4333-8636-5

All rights reserved. This book or any portion thereof may not be reproduced or used in any manner whatsoever without the express written permission of the author and publisher except for the use of brief quotations in a book review.

This is the *realest* and most down-to-earth introvert book you'll ever read. It's for every quiet person who has ever been asked "Why are you so quiet?" You'll finally have a worthy response after reading this book.

Dedication

This book is dedicated to God for creating me as an introvert, and for helping me to inspire others with my discovery. To my Mum for the love and support, Dad for the introverted genes, Ada, Toya, and Bibi, my very social siblings that made all these experiences possible —I love you guys!

AM I TOO QUIET?

From the Author

"Learning about introversion, especially if you're an introvert, doesn't only improve your intellect but helps you stay on top of your game 'constantly'. You'll feel more at peace with yourself and can effectively channel your quiet energy into productive sources."

— Yadirichi Oyibo, Author.

Content

No, there's nothing wrong with you. 1
The Origin Of This Mindset 2
Breaking the Negative Stereotypes About Introversion. 5
Essential Factors to Note About Introversion 10

Understanding the Science Behind Your Personality 17
What is an Introvert? 18
Causes of Introversion 20
Does Your Personality Change Over Time? 29

The Different Levels Of Introversion (& How to Deal with Extreme Introversion) 33
The Extroverts 34
The Introverted Extroverts 35
The Extreme Introverts 35
Your Sweet Spot 41
Chronicles 42

Leveraging Your Purpose as an Introvert (Where You'll Feel the Most Comfortable) — 51
- What does sweet spot mean? — 52
- Finding your purpose — 54
- Chronicles — 60

Active Steps to Using Your Quietness to Your Advantage — 63
- Understand yourself completely. — 64
- Focus on your strengths. — 65
- Set realistic expectations, but don't settle. — 66
- Record your successes. — 68

Final Words — 71

One

Chapter One

No, there's nothing wrong with you.

This chapter takes an enlightening look at one of the most challenging thought patterns introverts tend to have. We often feel there's something wrong with us, or that our quietness means we have a problem. If you've ever been in this position, then this book is for you.

We'll journey from the origin of this mindset to why it isn't plausible, even though people keep passing it on. Next, we'll learn some exciting facts about the introverted personality, which will make you more confident about yourself.

Overall, this chapter will help you acknowledge some negative mindsets about introversion, and how to fix it as soon as possible.

The Origin Of This Mindset

"You're too quiet!"

"Can you speak up a little bit?"

"You need to express yourself more often!"

"Are you shy?"

"You need to change your personality!"

No, There's Nothing Wrong With You.

Have you ever heard these phrases before? If you have, then you're most likely an introvert. We live in an extroverted world, where outgoing people get a chunk of the social cake. On the downside, introverts are often on the receiving end of negative backlash.

The origin of the mindset that *there's something wrong with you* is instilled by others who have a problem with introverted characters. Since introversion is one of the most misunderstood personalities, people often don't want to accommodate it, and will try their *very* best to change people with its traits.

However, this scenario doesn't indicate that there's something vividly wrong with you. If you pay close attention to your temperaments, you'll observe that you feel the most comfortable doing certain introverted tasks but tend to doubt yourself when others impose their opinions on you.

If your negative thought patterns come from external sources, teaching your inner critic how to filter the good from the bad can help you enjoy your quiet life even more. However, before you can learn how to silence other people's negativity, you have to first grow accustomed to your personality.

Learning more about introversion, especially if you're an introvert, doesn't just improve your intellect —but it helps you stay on top of your game *constantly*. You'll feel more at peace with yourself and can channel your energy into more productive sources.

Thankfully, this book provides just that, and in the next few chapters, you'll get the courage to be the most confident quiet person in the room.

Breaking the Negative Stereotypes About Introversion.

The first step we need to take as introverts before we can enjoy the quiet life is to destroy the stereotypical ideologies other people have about us —and the ones we have about ourselves too.

I grew up with most of these thought patterns and always thought other people were better suited than me. However, once I could conquer and defeat these damaging views, I instantly became liberated.

Here are three common stereotypes introverts need to change, especially if they've ever thought, "Am I too quiet?"

1. *You are weird or strange.*

The way other people perceive introverts can often make them think that they're strange. I used to ask myself, "Why am I so different from others?" Surely, being this quiet meant that there was something internally wrong with me. I tried my best to fit in, but the more I did, the more I experienced burnout.

As different or strange as you may feel, introverts make up approximately twenty-five to forty percent of the worldwide population. It means that introverts are everywhere. There might even be one sitting right next to you.

So, no! You're not weird, neither did you drop from outer space. Soft-spoken people are in every nook and cranny, and if you doubt that, you're reading one's book presently (me). The moment you realize that there are more people like you, you'll become more comfortable being yourself.

Understand that many introverts know how to blend into social settings. If you're worried that you're too different from others, there's a plus side to that. It means that you're too unique, and wouldn't compromise your genuineness merely to fit in with others. Your inability to fit in is a sign of how authentic you are.

2. *Introverts hate people.*

Another common negative stereotype that many people have passed on over the years is that introverts hate people. However, there's a difference between being antisocial and needing alone time. Antisocial people often have a *choice* on whether to socialize or not, while introverts naturally focus within and have less time for interaction.

An antisocial person might have the energy to connect with others but may choose not to. Introverts, on the other hand, tend to face burnout or sensory overload when engaging in social activities for too long. That's why we prefer to only make purposeful connections to reduce our workload.

This process is also deeply linked to how our brains are wired (more of that in chapter two). We might want to be the most extroverted person in the room, but we often get tired even before we can fulfill half of our expectations.

The idea that introverts hate people often makes us feel guilty when we turn down social invitations or leave gatherings sooner than expected. However, you shouldn't feel bad for your natural temperaments.

You're not a terrible person merely because you can't attend every party you're invited to. Therefore, this stereotype isn't valid.

3. *Introverts can't be successful because of their quiet traits.*

One of the major reasons why people tend to have a negative perception of introversion is because they feel it's a limiting personality in itself. "How can anyone ever truly achieve their dreams if they can't even come out of their shell?" people often think.

However, this is a terrible way to view introversion. Just because you can't do what every other person is doing doesn't make you a failure. Your quiet personality merely indicates that you have separate skills and talents from other folks.

This point is expressly discussed in my book, *Activate the Hidden Power of Your Introversion, (2020)*, where I talked about some of the greatest minds, which were, ironically, introverted. From Albert Einstein to Bill Gates and Elon Musk, there's a lot of evidence that shows introversion isn't a limiting personality.

It's necessary to stop competing in the social sphere of extroverts and dominate your niche like a pro. Eliminating the mindset that your personality will limit you from greatness is a critical step for all introverts. Understand that if you work as hard as anyone else, and more so, *wisely*, you can truly attain success.

Essential Factors to Note About Introversion

1. It's not a personality you can change.

I'm sorry, guys! I wished for this point not to be true several years ago, but the more I geared towards change, the more my true personality emerged. However, the inability of introverts to change isn't just theoretical. There's actual science behind why it's somewhat impossible.

According to research, the brains of introverts are different from extroverts. Factors like the release of dopamine and the activeness of our frontal cortex, which is responsible for decision-making, contribute to why introverts behave the way they do.

Unless you can vividly reconstruct your brain to operate much differently, there's not much you can do about your introverted traits except to leverage its strengths. You shouldn't spend too much time thinking about changing it, but take active measures to discover what makes you unique.

Knowing this factor alone should give you the confidence to dispel negative comments about you coming out of your shell. More so, you now have the opportunity to live a more fulfilling life.

2. *You're as loud as anyone else, just within.*

"You hardly ever talk!" People say.

'You should listen to what's happening in my head!' I murmur to myself.

If you've ever felt inferior for not being the *loud type*, remember that you're just as talkative as everyone else —except that people can't hear it. This factor should help you realize that there's nothing indeed wrong with you. You just have an introspective composition that allows you to focus internally more than you do outwardly.

The plus side to this trait is that it comes with a high level of prudence. Your thoughts are intricately processed before they get to your mouth, helping you harness your creativity even more. However, on

No, There's Nothing Wrong With You.

a platter, you and extroverts tend to speak the same amount of words, just not the same way.

An extrovert might channel their words externally but introverts prefer to keep theirs within. Sometimes, soft-spoken people prefer to be comfortable first before revealing what's inside. This is why some introverts might seem outgoing when they're in the right company.

If anyone has ever made you feel inferior for talking less when in public, remember that you're just as energetic as everyone else, but with a different channel of expression.

3. *You're wired differently.*

One key factor we've already established is that introverts and extroverts don't have the same internal wiring. Think of this explanation like an organization with respective departments. If everyone was fighting for the same position, the company wouldn't work.

Likewise, introverts and extroverts are wired differently because their purposes are distinct from each other (more about purpose in chapter four). Therefore, you should never feel bad for being quieter than your peers. Think of it this way —if everyone was talkative and outgoing in the world today, who would pay attention to the little details as much as you do?

According to research, introverts that pretend to be outgoing experience slower cognitive response rates, because their brains have to adjust their workings to something unusual. Therefore, trying to be like someone else only limits your productivity instead of plainly being yourself.

Always remember that you have a unique place in the world. Although many people may not realize it, your personality brings balance to the earth's systems. If you deviate from your true personality, you unknowingly create an imbalance that might be too tricky to figure out or solve. Therefore, never be afraid to be yourself, dear introvert.

Two

Chapter Two

Understanding the Science Behind Your Personality

In the previous chapter, we talked about why there's nothing wrong with being an introvert. More so, we highlighted why it's important to learn about your personality type because it helps you bask in your authentic self. While those theories are great, it's also important to look at things from a practical viewpoint.

Understanding the science about your personality gives you even more assurance of your uniqueness. Peradventure you forget about the conceptual side of your personality, knowing these aspects will be a reliable backup anytime, any day.

What is an Introvert?

An introvert is a person who focuses primarily on their thoughts rather than what's happening externally. Such a person might enjoy spending time alone rather than being in a crowd.

The words *introvert* and *extrovert* were coined by a Psychologist named Carl Jung in 1920. Although there's a common misconception that introverts are shy and always quiet, Carl Jung's theory of introversion relates to how people gain and dispel energy.

An introvert needs to focus within to gain their energy while extroverts depend on other people to fuel their inner vitality. Likewise, introverts tend to spend their energy in less-stimulating environments, while the opposite is the case for outgoing folks.

The theory of introversion and extroversion according to Carl Jung is relative to a person's inner workings rather than external factors (more on that later).

Signs of Introversion

- You get drained when you're around plenty of people.
- You enjoy having alone time/solitude.
- Others refer to you as *quiet*.
- You have a small tight-knit group of friends.
- People often find it difficult to read you from afar.
- You love to observe.
- You prefer working alone than working in groups.

Causes of Introversion

Many factors affect whether people turn out to be introverts or extroverts. Since most introverts tend to question their identity and the origin of their personality, it's essential to outline the most prominent causes of introversion.

Although there's no proven reason why people are introverts, there have been several studies over the years to explain this occurrence. Here are some of the concrete reasons why you might be an introvert.

1. Genetics

According to research, most people turn out to be introverted because it's in their genes. If they have a soft-spoken family member, some of their quiet traits can be passed on. Since the population of introverts is estimated to be around twenty-five to forty percent, there's a good chance that most families have introverts.

Therefore, if introversion is somewhere in your bloodline, it explains why you're the quiet type. In most cases, you don't have to live with an introverted family member before you can have their traits. Some hereditary factors are buried in your DNA irrespective of proximity.

From personal experience, I grew up in an extroverted household but still turned out profoundly introverted. Even though I didn't spend much time with my dad, I managed to get his introverted genes.

In a nutshell, many factors make up a person's temperament, and your DNA is undoubtedly one of them.

2. Environmental Factors.

An individual's environment can also affect whether they turn out to be introverts or extroverts. This process occurs because a person's environment can condition them to think in a certain way. Although this factor may not be the sole cause of everyone's introversion, it's still potent.

For example, things like parenting style can affect whether a child is comfortable outdoors or at ease with others. If a parent is overprotective, the child might grow up to dislike social interaction, further building their introverted traits.

Other factors that go hand in hand with environmental factors include the type of education a person receives, their childhood and life experiences, or encounters with their peers. For example, someone who has been constantly mistreated will find comfort in spending time alone rather than with others.

Even so, if a person's occupation requires them to be quiet and more observant, they'll gradually adapt to these temperaments the longer they practice them.

3. *Your brain.*

Lastly, as Carl Jung explained, the above-listed personality types differ based on people's mental workings. The way your brain operates might be the reason for your introverted personality.

If you're sensitive to external stimuli, you might be an introvert. However, if your brain thrives on the excitement of the outside world, you might be extroverted.

Let's take a look at some key terms that showcase the difference between the brains of introverts and extroverts.

- *Dopamine and acetylcholine.*

These are the *feel-good* neurotransmitters. Dopamine is a compound found in the brain that acts as a neurotransmitter (it sends messages from one brain cell to another).

The body naturally releases this compound as a reward to help individuals feel excited when taking several actions. This compound is mostly released in response to quick actions and can make an individual feel pumped to repeat the same action.

Acetylcholine is also a rewarding chemical in the brain. It's a neurotransmitter that responds to subtler acts and can make a person feel more relaxed and content with the activities they do.

Understanding the Science Behind Your Personality.

Interestingly, introverts are shockingly more sensitive to dopamine than extroverts. The response their brain gives to this chemical is like a child being overfed with candy. The more you give them, the more they feel sick.

This process explains why introverts might feel overstimulated when in certain social settings. It's not that they don't enjoy the scenario, but their brain can't have so much of it, or it would feel like a sickness. According to research, introverts respond better to the neurotransmitter, Acetylcholine, which is why they prefer subtler and calmer activities.

As you've guessed, the reverse is the case for extroverts. They thrive on dopamine, and it perpetually makes them pumped for more activities. Their brains don't easily get weary from this rewarding chemical, which is why they seem to have more mental energy for social encounters.

- *Blood Flow and Gray Matter.*

Several studies have shown that introverts tend to have more blood flow to their brains than extroverts. Specifically, these researches show that soft-spoken people have increased blood flow to their frontal lobe, which is the area responsible for remembering, planning, and decision making.

This discovery explains why introverts tend to focus more within than externally. An increased amount of blood flow to the brain indicates more internal activity. Even so, Broca's area, which is responsible for self-talk, is prone to be more active in introverts than extroverts.

More neural activity suggests lesser outward stimulation. It's also the reason why introverts tend to be burned out by dopamine faster than extroverts. Their inner workings are already so busy that they can't afford more outward fuel.

Introverts also use the sympathetic side of their brains more than their parasympathetic sides —unlike extroverts. The sympathetic side releases the neurotransmitter acetylcholine, which helps them to relax, while the parasympathetic side fuels their dopamine.

Since introverts tend to have increased blood flow to certain areas of their brain, another research suggests this process to be the reason they have thicker gray matter. The gray matter is located in the prefrontal cortex which is the area of the brain responsible for cognitive functions and abstract thinking.

- *Acetylcholine vs. Dopamine Pathway.*

As previously mentioned, the neurotransmitter Acetylcholine provides comfort to a person, while Dopamine gets you pumped for more activities. Interestingly, there are pathways in the brain where these compounds transport themselves. People often refer to them as the Acetylcholine and Dopamine pathways.

Several researches were conducted on both introverts and extroverts to analyze how they processed information. Scientists injected them with doses of radioactivity and discovered that the brains of introverts and extroverts took different pathways to transport information, and had different timeframes.

In extroverts, the information passed through the Dopamine pathway, but for the soft-spoken person, it passed through the Acetylcholine pathway. Surprisingly, the Acetylcholine pathway takes a longer time to reach the brain, which explains the introverts' high level of brain activity. Even so, more time to process information also reveals an introvert's tendency to overthink and process circumstances thoroughly.

With all these activities happening in your head, know that you're more unique than you realize. These discoveries should also help you feel better about your personality type.

Does Your Personality Change Over Time?

Introverts are often pressured by others to change their personality. Some might even tell stories of how they were much more introverted before but learned to overcome their social difficulties.

Although there are impressive stories of people either becoming more extroverted or introverted, the real question introverts want to know is, "Can my personality change over time?"

The three major factors listed above that influence a person's personality are genetics, environment, and a person's brain. These are both internal and external factors that can affect a person's temperament.

External factors such as the environment can cause significant changes in a person's character. People tend to adapt to new circumstances as they get older and might possibly conquer some of their fears. However, some internal factors are likely not to change.

Therefore, a person can learn to be more sociable to others, but would still prefer having alone time because of how their brain functions. Their personality didn't change, but they learned to adapt to their environment.

You can train yourself to manage certain environmental factors, but if you try to change your inner workings, you will only limit your productivity.

Understanding the Science Behind Your Personality.

Therefore, the answer to the former question is, *no*. You can't change your personality, but you can learn to adapt to new circumstances.

Three

Chapter Three

The Different Levels Of Introversion (& How to Deal with Extreme Introversion)

According to Carl Jung (the founder of analytical psychology), introversion and extroversion are a spectrum of characteristics where people have a combination of both traits in different degrees.

This notion suggests that people aren't just introverts and extroverts, but a union of the two. It also means that even extroverts have a little bit of introversion, and vice versa. For example, an extrovert might be seventy percent extroverted and thirty percent introverted.

However, some people tend to have extreme temperaments. Now let's take a look at the different levels of introversion in people, and how it affects their dealings in the world.

- **The Extroverts**

Extroverts are on the further end of the spectrum and tend to have more sociable traits. However, this factor doesn't suggest the absence of introversion. Extroverts still face downtimes when they've been in social settings for too long. The only difference is that it takes them longer to reach this stage.

The Different Levels of Introversion.

- ## *The Introverted Extroverts*

Introverted extroverts have a blend of the two traits and are in the middle of this spectrum. These individuals are otherwise referred to as ambiverts and might seem like extroverts in one scene while displaying introverted qualities in another.

People in this category tend to enjoy the best of both worlds. They can maximize their potential in social settings but still use their introverted strengths to their advantage.

- ## *The Extreme Introverts*

These are people with deeply introverted traits at the beginning of the spectrum. They tend to face burnout quicker than others, and often feel out of place in social environments. While they might struggle with socializing, these individuals tend to unravel some of the deepest hidden abilities that shock the world.

The Dilemma of Extreme Introverts

As you've guessed, this book is tailored to people that might ask themselves, "Am I too quiet?" — which are extreme introverts. While there are many benefits of being a predominantly introverted person, there are still several challenges we tend to face.

It's essential to discuss some of the things that undoubtedly limit us, so that we can learn how to use our introversion to our advantage. Here are some struggles extreme introverts face, and how to solve them.

The Different Levels of Introversion.

1. *Constantly feeling inferior.*

The feeling of inferiority is a major struggle for deep introverts. The way others perceive a high state of introversion tends to affect the way we see ourselves. You might have an excellent time basking in your hidden strengths without external opinion. However, when people believe you have a problem or ask why you don't talk often, you would inevitably start thinking there's something wrong with you.

Thankfully, we've given many reasons why this opinion is futile in the first chapter. You can always reread it anytime you're feeling down. But, know that you can't always educate everyone about your temperaments. There'll always be that *one* person that wouldn't *get* you and would wish you were more like them.

I've learned over the years that building personal confidence is the best way to handle being an extreme introvert. You don't necessarily need everyone to know what makes you different. You need to know these things for yourself.

The irony about this situation is that everyone has a dose of introverted qualities to some degree. However, having prominent introverted qualities doesn't make you inferior, it makes you just as good as everyone else.

2. *A strong desire to socialize.*

While deep introverts enjoy solitude much more than others, they tend to get carried away by its comfort to the extent they forget there's a life outside of it. Deep introverts realize this fact when they have a strong urge to talk to someone, but there aren't many options.

The first thing to know about being in such a situation is that there's nothing wrong with having few friends or none at all. Being an extreme

The Different Levels of Introversion.

introvert doesn't make you antisocial —it means you're *selectively* social, and that's an excellent life choice. Even though you're more comfortable with your small friendship circle, you shouldn't also feel limited by it.

You can have as many friends as you desire, but you unconsciously realize that these friendships might drain or add no value to your life. Making friends isn't impossible for you, but you've made a wise, subliminal decision to stick to purposeful ones. This realization would always help you find balance in tough situations.

Another way to handle this dilemma is to realize that sometimes, you might have the urge to socialize, while for the most part, you won't —and that's also fine. Never be too hard on yourself in either of the situations. Whenever you need to enjoy solitude, do it to the best of your ability; and whenever you feel the need to talk to someone, enjoy the awkwardness of leaving your comfort zone.

Being an extreme introvert means you'll inevitably face some *extremes*. Never beat yourself up for being too quiet, neither should you have the mindset that you're too awkward or introverted to desire friendships or to build them.

3. Struggling to fit in.

Another prominent dilemma extreme introverts face is their inability to fit in. We might think we have a disorder, but it's merely because we spend more time in their heads than most people. Extreme introverts have a rich inner world that they crave to explore constantly. Most of their strengths and potentials need a great amount of solitude to discover, which can greatly decrease their time for socializing.

The Different Levels of Introversion.

However, identifying your purpose and relishing in what makes you special and more valuable to the world will help you thrive as an extreme introvert. In clearer terms, you won't be living your life to please others, but you'll find the most comfortable way to fulfill your dreams.

That's the secret to living an introverted life and truly enjoying it. The pressure from the world to be more outgoing will always be there. But, you can learn to manage several difficulties by finding your *sweet spot*.

Your sweet spot is;

- the area you're the most productive without putting in too much effort,
- where you can harness your hidden strengths,
- the silent area you'll be grateful for the introvert that you are.

Thankfully, all of these are discussed in the next chapter.

Chronicles

- *Elle*

Elle was an extreme introvert that enjoyed solitude. She enjoyed writing, reading, and more often than most, watching YouTube videos. Elle enjoyed doing these things because it helped her experience the world from the comfort of her bedroom.

Although Elle enjoyed the quiet life, she occasionally faced the dilemma of feeling inferior (the first struggle). People often told her that she was too quiet, and to *an annoying extent*, as they'd put it.

The Different Levels of Introversion.

They also tried to get close to her, but her desire to be alone often pushed them away. Many people couldn't penetrate her quiet nature, despite how alluring she seemed from afar.

With time, Elle began to ponder on their grievances. She believed that she had a problem because no one seemed to be as quiet as she was. Perhaps, she was *over-doing* it, she would think to herself.

Elle decided to make personal research since she had no one else to confide in. She read several journals on introversion and found out that a significant amount of the world's population was just like her. Her confidence grew the more she read about her personality. She also joined some online forums and connected with people who understood her.

She was getting more comfortable in her own skin, but she still couldn't convince everyone that there was nothing wrong with her. She decided to stick with the purposeful friends she had instead of trying to please everyone.

Even though people still complained about her disposition, their statements didn't matter as much anymore. She wore her head up high and chose to refrain from arguing with people that just didn't *get* it.

- **Sharon.**

Sharon was an extreme introvert who enjoyed expressing herself through art. She spent many hours with her drawing equipment, and it helped her enjoy the comfort of solitude.

Although Sharon went to college for four years, she didn't have a best friend. She communicated with several people but didn't have someone close enough to confide in. For the most part, she wasn't bothered about her lack of friends. She could

The Different Levels of Introversion.

always talk to her family members whenever something dire arose.

However, during some downtimes, Sharon often felt a strong urge to socialize (the second struggle). She didn't want to rely on only her siblings for social support. She wanted to have the full college experience, and truly be independent.

Anytime Sharon felt this way, she would feel bad about being introverted. She would wish for a more outgoing spirit so that she could enjoy the beauty of the ever-social world. On one of those days, Sharon decided to take a bold step.

She realized that many people previously attempted to get close to her, but she turned them down by choosing solitude over socializing unconsciously. She hastily reached back to some of them and planned some meetups.

This action was against her principles, but there was a sense of exhilaration that accompanied deliberately meeting with others for the first time. She felt like a normal person and was excited to finally build deep connections with people.

Hours into those get-togethers, Sharon's social battery kept running down. She enjoyed talking for the first few minutes but soon wanted to retreat into her comfort zone. She knew it wasn't because of her introverted tendencies because she could talk to her siblings for hours without feeling tired.

After much thought, Sharon then realized that deep purposeful connections couldn't be forced. She had always known this, but she didn't decipher early enough that her sudden desire to talk to people was merely casual. There was nothing wrong with that, but she mistook it for something more profound, and was handling things the wrong way.

The Different Levels of Introversion.

This misunderstanding arose because she had certain insecurities about having no close friendships. Therefore, she was trying to fix her problem at all costs.

Sharon loved the experience of meeting people but realized that she needed to manage her spontaneous urges better. More so, she needed to understand herself more.

The first thing she realized from that encounter was that she wasn't too introverted to connect with people. Her preference for a smaller social circle was because she desired to find valuable connections, and having few didn't mean she was defective. It meant she was a thoughtful introvert.

Secondly, she realized that she could benefit more from the little conversations she had with people rather than wanting to connect deeply with everyone. More so, trying to go against her natural temperament would only cause her more burnout.

Sharon later became self-assured about her personality. She understood herself more each day, and was loving every self-discovery process she embarked on.

Four

Chapter Four

Leveraging Your Purpose as an Introvert (Where You'll Feel the Most Comfortable)

The world tends to constantly put pressure on soft-spoken folks because of the misconception that outgoing people have more opportunities to be successful. However, many successful introverts in today's world have graciously left the sphere of social pressure because they found where they were most effective. In other words, they found their sweet spots.

What does sweet spot mean?

The word *sweet spot,* according to the Cambridge dictionary, is the part of a surface that gives the most power for the least effort. It could be the point or area of a bat or club that makes the most useful contact with a ball.

Humans relatively have their sweet spots too. These are areas we feel more comfortable and effective without trying too much. For extroverts, their vibrant persona makes the world believe that anything can be easy for them. But for introverts, it can be difficult for others to perceive our strongest points.

Finding your sweet spot isn't about proving to the world that you can accomplish your goals. It's about

Leveraging Your Purpose as an Introvert.

dominating your niche without having to unhealthily compete with others. This process will affect the way you view your personality, and would ultimately affect the way others see you.

People like Bill Gates, Keanu Reeves, Elon Musk, Emma Watson, and Mark Zuckerberg all found their sweet spots despite being introverts. The world doesn't pressure them to be extroverts because they've convinced everyone that success isn't limited to a personality type.

Know that people won't necessarily know when you've found your sweet spot. But, thriving in it will undoubtedly affect your mindset. For the most part, you'll have a silent response when people say you're too quiet, and you'll no longer feel pressured to be like everyone else.

Finding your purpose

You might be wondering, "What does purpose even mean, and how is it linked to finding your *sweet spot?*" As previously mentioned, the world has a balance of outgoing and reserved personalities for a reason. *Purpose* means the distinct role everyone plays to make the world well-suited. The word *world* here can also indicate your immediate surroundings, or in general, your life.

Finding your purpose can make your life as an introvert even more splendid. This process connotes understanding the distinct reason why you're better off as an introvert than any other personality you could try to imitate. After this step, you can easily point out your sweet spot.

The first thing to realize before searching for your purpose is that all introverts are different. Since introversion and extroversion are a spectrum of traits where anyone can fall at any end of the range, you should realize that your character is distinct.

With many resources today, we can thankfully see how diverse the introverted personality truly is. Paying attention to what makes you different from everyone else, even severe factors like being too quiet, can help you know where your hidden strengths lie.

Below are some steps to take if you want to find your purpose and relish in your sweet spot:

- *Renovate your mindset.*

The essence of every chapter thus far has been to change your perception of introversion to a positive view. You can only thrive well as an introvert if you believe that your personality is indeed beautiful.

It's also crucial to separate some of your flaws from the characteristics of introversion. For example, being an introvert might make you self-sufficient, but refraining from asking for help even when you need it isn't a trait of introversion. It's something you might grow accustomed to due to your reserved tendencies.

If such a behavior limits you, it's crucial to work on it without desiring to change your personality as a whole. Once you separate your limiting traits from your personality, you can thrive better and unravel your most productive assets.

- *Pay attention to your comfort zone.*

You need to monitor the activities you engage in during solitude. It could be writing, reading, drawing, or simply harnessing your creativity. Whatever makes you comfortable can expose you to some of your hidden strengths. It's crucial to capitalize on these areas because they'll make you feel more confident about your personality type in the long run.

Another benefit of paying attention to your comfort zone is that it helps you know how to recharge. When you inevitably experience burnout from social situations, you'll need an activity you can easily turn to in order to gain mental strength.

Know that the more time you spend boosting your mental and social energy is the more you can function better in the world. Always remember that adequate *alone time* equals being a happy, productive introvert.

- *Inspire others.*

There's something undoubtedly refreshing about making an impact with what you do. It's both beneficial to you and the receiver. More so, it's one of the littlest ways to validate that your personality isn't a limitation but a global force.

For example, if you love to draw, you can gift some people with your art to brighten up their day. If you enjoy reading books, you can create a space recommending some of your favorite stories. There are seemingly many ways introverts can make an impact by expressing the profoundness of their inner world (more of that in the next chapter).

More so, you'll have a valid response whenever someone asks, "Why are you so quiet?" The silent smile you put on people's faces will validate your need for so much solitude.

You can still work a nine-to-five job or run a successful business while striving to make the most of your hidden abilities. It's one of the keys to living a fulfilled introverted life. If you neglect your quiet tendencies and only engage in other activities that unconsciously wear you out, you'll dislike your personality even more. On the contrary, sharing your introverted strengths with the world in the most comfortable way, helps you and others to see how unique you truly are.

- *Be authentic.*

You might be similar to other introverts, but you're peculiar in your own way. Being authentic helps you radiate something so distinct that the world, and even yourself, can't dispute.

It's crucial to remember that your authenticity is what no one can take away from you. As you focus on embracing solitude and inspiring others in the process, it's essential to stick to what makes you different. These are the unique parts of your voice, perspective, or story, that make you stand out in the midst of many.

Chronicles

- *Jack*

Jack was a pretty quiet fellow who enjoyed listening to music and exploring the depth of human nature. He also enjoyed cooking and seemed to find his place in the kitchen.

Jack worked a full-time job and made a substantial income but he didn't seem too pleased with his life. Like many introverts, he believed that he was too different and couldn't make worthwhile connections. Jack cooked meals to feel better about his temperament during his leisure time. However, he was constantly reminded about his isolated life whenever he was back at work.

He repeated this routine every weekend until he decided to do something different. He casually posted his cooking tactics online, and a good amount of people were amazed by his viewpoint. Even so, they started requesting to see more on his personal judgement on recipes and cooking tips.

He embraced his unfeigned self each time he decided to inspire people with his culinary knowledge. He wasn't doing it merely because someone else was doing it, but because cooking made him happy, and he wanted to share that joy unconsciously. More so, he ensured he expressed himself to the degree he was comfortable with.

During that process, he realized that he didn't have a problem connecting with people. He merely needed to find his sweet spot by first finding out what he loved doing. He then used cooking as an avenue to feel better, recharge, and also to connect with others. More so, it helped him understand the unique role he played as an introvert in the world, and why didn't need to change to be more effective.

Five

Chapter Five

Active Steps to Using Your Quietness to Your Advantage

The previous chapters have explained in detail why you don't have a deficient character but a powerful one. Peradventure you're struggling to fit everything into actionable steps, this chapter will help you accomplish that. If you want to make the most of your quiet life, below are three essential stages you need to go through.

- *Understand yourself completely.*

We've previously established that you're unique, even as an introvert. A great amount of the world's population tends to have a mixture of introverted and extroverted traits. This means that people on the far ends like extreme introverts and extreme extroverts might find it hard to fit in.

Nevertheless, the first step to conquering the introverted life is to realize that you're unique. Apart from having a distinct range of characteristics, other factors like your culture, family background, personal beliefs, and experiences, tend to make you different from every other introvert out there. Therefore, it's crucial to understand what solely works for you.

Treat yourself like a rare entity on planet earth, instead of categorizing yourself with others. This process will help you identify the necessary actions

Using Your Quietness to Your Advantage.

you need to take to make your life more comfortable. It could be spending more time in solitude when you feel like it, or pacifying your desire to communicate with others.

If you don't spend enough time observing your temperaments, you might easily fall victim to the pressures of the world. Even so, you won't be able to find your sweet spot and truly live a happy introverted life.

- *Focus on your strengths.*

It's crucial to establish that you won't be great at everything all introverts thrive in. That's because every quiet person has a unique set of abilities that helps them stand out. Nevertheless, focus on your strengths and find your unique voice alongside. This process will help you stay as authentic as you can be.

It doesn't matter if other people can do the same things that you do. Your distinct personality will help your output remain unparalleled. Pay attention to the things you're great at, and you'll appreciate your quiet qualities even better.

Another key strategy to help you focus on your strengths is to avoid comparing yourself to others. Your weakness might be another person's strength and vice versa. Spend enough time in solitude so that you can tap into the happiness your hidden strengths provide. The more you can exploit the benefits of being an introvert every day, the more thrilling your life will become.

- *Set realistic expectations, but don't settle.*

As you try to make the most of your hidden abilities, it's necessary to set goals you can achieve. You can do this by paying attention to your

Using Your Quietness to Your Advantage.

individual character. For example, if you feel a sudden desire to leave your comfort zone, try not to start with extreme adventures. Always try to contain your anticipation to avoid complete burnout.

However, the most essential thing remains to find a balance with every action you take. You might get things right, or you might get them wrong. Nevertheless, try not to do too much, or to do nothing at all. In the end, you'll eventually find out what works for you.

Another thing to note is that many people will inevitably try to make you feel inferior for being an introvert. The best way to curb the pressure is to avoid settling for less. Popular knowledge often dictates that introverts are good at some things and bad at others. However, unless you try out several ideas, you can never truly explore your hidden self.

Try not to belittle your qualities to what people think about you. If you have an interest in specific areas, ensure you go for them. The journey to self-discovery starts with a single step. If you eventually dislike the results, you'd have at least learned something new about yourself. And that, in itself, is more powerful than anything you can imagine.

Know that you shouldn't always remain in your comfort zone, and you should also avoid putting excessive pressure on yourself. In a nutshell, set goals based on your tendencies, but never be complacent with less than you can achieve.

- *Record your successes.*

You'll never know how far you've come until you document your successes. While you're trying to discover what works best for you, it's crucial to pay attention to your progress.

Using Your Quietness to Your Advantage.

Record the things you accomplished effortlessly, and also the activities that made you immensely happy. You may not need to keep repeating these actions. But, seeing how far you've come will motivate you to keep on conquering. You'll also realize that you're not as limited as you perceive yourself to be.

Six

Chapter Six

Final Words

Two major factors can limit you from using your quietness to your advantage: people's opinions and your mind.

People won't always be the best judge of character. It's essential to realize that a lot of individuals are undereducated about the diversity of personalities and tend to feel everyone should fit into certain standards. However, the world works better with a balance of traits.

Acknowledging this fact will help you dispute some of the negative comments people would make about your personality. It's also essential to overcome your limiting traits but not to envision your personality as the problem.

The second thing that can limit you is your mind. Once you unconsciously absorb the opinions of others, you might conclude that there's something wrong with you. You'll also start craving a more outgoing nature, so that you can live your life without limits.

Anytime you feel this way, it's crucial to remember that even extroverts have a hard time figuring out their lives. Their temperaments don't guarantee automatic success. Likewise, becoming more sociable won't ascertain instant results for you.

Final Words

Every individual needs to put in an ample amount of effort to attain success —whether they're introverts or extroverts. Never believe that you're too constrained to triumph. Limitation often starts with a person's thoughts, so try your best to think positively about yourself.

What next?

You've made it this far, so you're probably wondering what your next line of action should be. Here's a quick rundown of where you can start:

- Start a self-discovery process by paying attention to your unique temperaments and documenting what works best for you.

- Acknowledge your strengths and weaknesses, but don't use them against yourself. More so, don't try to compare them with others because you're a unique being with distinctive characters.

- Always tackle your negative thoughts and learn to think positively about yourself.

- Embrace solitude, not only as a way to recharge, but to find out your hidden strengths.

- Document your adventures and accomplishments. You'll never know how exciting your introvert life truly is until you start the habit of personal reflection.

- Find out how to use your hidden strengths to communicate with the world. This process will help you realize your sweet spot.

- Never stop trying. You might win at some, and lose at others. Nevertheless, every action aids the self-realization process.

- Disconnect from people who might constantly make you feel inferior for being an introvert.

More so, never feel bad for putting yourself first, especially when it comes to your mental health.

- Lastly, always relish how amazing you are. You might be quiet but you add a deep, rich essence to the world even without knowing it. Keep on being you, dear introvert.

About the Author

Yadirichi Oyibo is the founder of Diary Of An Introvert, a blog that showcases a world inside every introvert's mind.

It all began with an idea - or rather, a journal. She wanted to document her experiences in this crazy extroverted world (and trust me, it was a rollercoaster experience), but she soon realized it was too profound to fit into her journal.

After many years of hovering around with the concept, she knew she needed to create a blog. And thus, Diary Of An Introvert was born with the sole aim to unite introverts all over the world with relatable experiences.

Final Words

Visit the home of introverts at www.diaryofanintrovertng.com or connect with Yadi via email at contact@diaryofanintrovertng.com or via her Instagram page @therealyadirichi.

Also by Yadirichi Oyibo

Activate the Hidden Power Of Your Introversion

Diary Of An Introvert: A 14-Week Introvert Journal

Resources

Aart-Coppes, M. (2013). The Introvert Brain Explained.

Carpenter, D. (2020). Tips for Increasing Your Happiness as an Introvert

Granneman, J. (2019). Introverts' and Extroverts' Brains Really Are Different, According to Science

Oyibo, Y. (2020). Activate the Hidden Power of Your Introversion.

Special thanks to you for making it to the end.

Made in the USA
Middletown, DE
24 June 2022